It's Castle Time!
A Kid's Guide To Dubrovnik, Croatia

Photography By John D. Weigand
Poetry By Penelope Dyan

Bellissima Publishing, LLC
Jamul, California
www.bellissimapublishing.com

copyright © 2011 by Penny D. Weigand and John D. Weigand

All rights reserved. No part of this book may be
reproduced or transmitted in any form or by any means,
electronic or mechanical, including photocopying,
recording, or by any other means, or by any information or
storage retrieval system, without permission from the publisher.

ISBN 978-1-61477-011-4
First Edition

Take a Walk!

It's Castle Time!
Bellissima Publishing, LLC

Introduction

Dubrovnik is a Croatian city on the Adriatic Sea coast, at the terminal end of the Isthmus of Dubrovnik. It is one of the most prominent tourist destinations on the Adriatic, a seaport and the centre of Dubrovnik-Neretva county. But this is not what is fascinating about this place. Kids and adults alike will marvel at what they see when they approach Dubrovnik, because what you see and what you find (kid's are very keen on exploring and finding things) is a walled city, a real bridge that goes over a moat and a drawbridge! And there is much, much more!

Photographer John D. Weigand and Penelope Dyan (attorney, award winning author, poet and former teacher) let you travel with them through the photographs and words of this book, not spoon feeding facts, but letting the eye capture a moment to stir an imagination. Learning is about exploration, and whether you explore through a book, or in person by visiting a place, kids see what the adult eye doesn't see. Dyan and Weigand follow the things that kids see, not adults. Kids are encouraged, as with all Dyan/Weigand travel books to make this book their own, to add to it, insert their own photographs, postcards and words. Learning should always be a personal thing.

It's Castle Time!
Bellissima Publishing, LLC

It's Castle Time!
A Kid's Guide To Dubrovnik, Croatia

Photography By John D. Weigand
Poetry By Penelope Dyan

There is a place surrounded
by a wall of stone,
where you'll never feel alone.
The blue of the sea melts
into the sky above.
It's Dubrovnik, Croatia,
a place filled with love.

You dream of queens,
of princes, princesses and kings.
You dream of glass slippers,
of croaking frogs saying "ribbit"
and of all sorts of things.
You walk toward a drawbridge,
on a bridge over a moat,
and in the water behind you
you hear the horn of a boat.

There is a majestic tower.

There are steps that lead to a "from the castle" view.

Splashing in the village fountain
(escaping the summer heat)
is another thing you can do!

When you look to your right.
Cannonballs come into sight.

And when you take a walk
down the village street,
the cobblestones skip
beneath your two feet.

Some narrow streets (of stairs) go straight up.
Other streets are flat and low.
Your dad says, "It's NOT about the street at all! It's about where YOU want to go!"

Laundry hangs from windows,
drying in the sun,
to be taken inside and folded,
before the day is done.

You can float in a kayak
in the blue of a sea,
that is as calm and as tranquil
as anything can be.
You paddle carefully between
the rocks,
once you leave Dubrovnik's
docks.

When you are finished kayaking, you walk right down the street.

Your Mom says, "Here's an
ice- cream store,
and you can have a treat!"
You are tired now and hungry.
(It's been quite a day.)
Soon you will leave this place,
to go meandering on your way.
You will dream about the
all the adventures lying ahead,
when on night's pillow
you lay your sweet head.

"Dream tonight of peacock tails, Diamond fields and spouter whales. Ills are many, blessing few, But dreams tonight will shelter you."

Herman Melville
August 1, 1819 – September 28, 1891

www.ingramcontent.com/pod-product-compliance
Lightning Source LLC
LaVergne TN
LVHW071652060526
838200LV00029B/435